Look at the Moon

From different lives, Bill, Sam, and Ben
see the same bright moon.   —B. G.

The illustrations for this book are collagraphs. A collagraph is made up of pieces of paper, fabric, string,
and other materials glued onto a plate of heavy cardboard. The plate is then inked and printed on an
etching press. When dry, watercolor washes are added to the print for color and highlights.

For information contact:
MONDO Publishing
980 Avenue of the Americas, New York, NY 10018

Printed in Hong Kong by South China Printing Co. (1988) Ltd.
99 00 01   9 8 7 6 5 4 3

Designed by Sylvia Frezzolini Severance
Production by Our House

Library of Congress Cataloging-in-Publication Data

Garelick, May, 1910-
    Look at the moon / May Garelick ; illustrated by Barbara Garrison.
       p.   cm.
    Summary: A journey in verse to discover whether the same moon shines
on all parts of the world.
       ISBN 1-57255-142-9 (hc : alk. paper). — ISBN 1-57255-141-0 (pbk : alk. paper)
       [1. Moon—Fiction. 2. Stories in rhyme.]   I. Garrison, Barbara, ill. II. Title.
PZ8.3.G18Lo   1996
[Fic]—dc20   95-49115
                                                                       CIP
                                                                       AC

Look at
the Moon

BY MAY GARELICK

IILLUSTRATED BY

BARBARA GARRISON

Moon light, moon bright,
Shining on this lovely night.
Does everyone see the moon I see,
The very same moon that shines on me?

Behind the barn, my black cat
Prowls in the light of the moon—
Silently stalking, hunting, pursuing.
Tell me, kitty cat, is the moon you see
The same as the moon that shines on me?

Deep in the woods
Moonbeams sparkle overhead
As the rays of moonlight silently spread,
Silvering the trees, the rushing streams,
Bathing the woods in glowing beams.

Night animals roam the woods.

An owl, a deer,

A wide-eyed raccoon.

An opossum here.

A rabbit there.

And somewhere, maybe even a bear.

Is the moon that shines on animals and trees

The same bright moon that my black cat sees?

Headlights, house lights,
Blazing bright street lights.
Red, white, and green lights.
Night in the city.

Does the moon shine on the city?
When I was there, I looked.
There was a moon all right.
But the city at night
Needs no moon to make it bright.

A sailor once told me
That out at sea,
The moon's reflection paves
A glowing path across the waves.

And when it is night
In a land across the sea,
The moon shines down on a chimpanzee
Half asleep in a jungle tree.

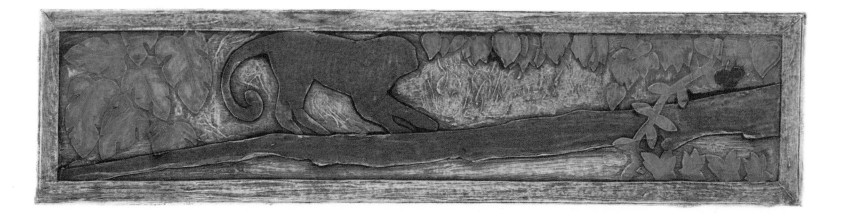

It shines on elephants
Tramping in single file.

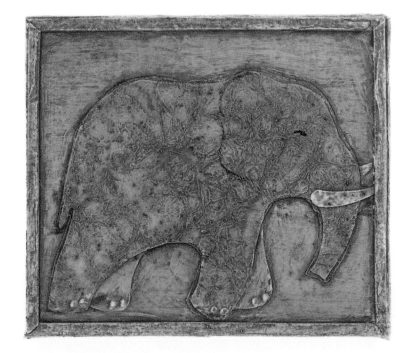

And in the waters of the Nile,
The moon shines
On the crocodile.

I wonder, though,
About the land of ice and snow.
Does the moon shine with a golden glow
On igloos, and on polar bears,
On caribou, and snowshoe hares?

And in another land,
Where kangaroos leap,
And koalas play,
They have night where we have day.
What about these places far away?
Do they have a moon?

Yes. When night comes,
And the skies are clear,
The moon shines there, as well as here.
Everywhere—
The same moon shines its quiet light
On farm and field and hill and hollow,
On trees of pine, and oak, and willow,
On cities, farms, and wooded hills,
On rooftops, and on window sills.

Once each month comes a special night
When the same moon shines full and bright,
Casting its light for all to see.
For you, and sailors,
For kitty cats, and me.

Moon light, moon bright,
Shining on a lovely night.
I'm glad that everyone in the world can see
The same full moon that shines on me.